The Blessing Seed

Barefoot Books

PO Box 95

Kingswood

Bristol BS15 5BH

ISBN 1 901223 70 1

The illustrations for this book were prepared in watercolour on paper.
The text was set in Bradley Hand.

Graphic design: Design/Section, Frome, Somerset, England
Reproduction: Scanner Services, Verona, Italy
Printed and bound in Singapore by Tien Wah Press

The Blessing Seed

A Creation Myth for the New Millennium

Written by Caitlin Matthews

illustrated by Alison Dexter

BAREFOOT BOOKS

BATH

In the beginning, God sang everything alive. God sang the

sky, the land and the seas. God sang the plants and trees.

God sang the moon, the sun and the stars.
God sang animals to live in the sea, in the sky

and on the Earth. Then God, Mother and Father of All, sang of Man and Woman.

God said to them, 'This Earth is your garden.
The rocks, plants, trees and animals are your family.
Go and explore your home.'

The Man and the Woman thanked God.
They greeted every stone, plant, tree and animal.
They learned what each living thing could do.

The Man and the Woman
found a tall tree in the
middle of the garden.
It had four paths
leading away
from it.
'What is this for?'
they asked God.
God said,
'That is the Tree
of Life.

On it grows the fruit of knowledge. But it isn't ripe yet, so you mustn't eat it. The four paths are ways to explore this world. When the fruit is ripe you will be able to walk them all.'

The Man and Woman
sat together and watched the stars
grow bright in the sky. Then the Woman
said to God, 'Everyone in the garden has their
special gift. The squirrel can jump, the snake can
crawl, the bird can fly. What is our special gift?'
And God answered, 'In all the world, you and the
Man are most like me.

You have a special duty.
You will care for everything on Earth.
Your special gift is to learn and to care.'
'How will we do that?' asked the Man.
'Listen for the song that I sang at the beginning,'
said God. 'My song is in everything and it will
help you to learn and to care.'

The Woman listened to the song of the Tree of Life. It sang a song of laughter, a song of tears, a song of beginning and a song of coming home. She said, 'Maybe I will understand our special gift if I eat the fruit?' She picked the fruit and tasted it. It was sweet and bitter, soft and sharp.

As she swallowed
it, things began to change.
She felt like a cloud looking
down on the land far below. The birds,
trees, animals and rocks felt far away.
She shared the fruit with the Man.
When he tasted it, he felt different
and frightened. 'Why do the
animals run away from
us?' he cried.

God came that evening and said,
'You are frightened and upset. Have you eaten the
fruit of the Tree of Life?'
The Man said, 'We did. And now the animals hide
from us. We don't understand what is different.'
The Woman said, 'We ate because we wanted to
discover our special gift.'
God smiled and said, 'I made mountains to last
forever. I made flowers and trees for beauty. I made
birds, fish and animals for their many gifts. But I
made human beings for their longing to know —
it is time for you to explore the four paths. Come!'

And God led them to the Tree of Life and showed them the paths, 'The four paths are called the path of wonder, the path of

emptiness, the path of making
and the path of coming home.
These four paths of life will help
you to learn and to care.

On the path of wonder, you will remember
when you were sung from the Earth.
When you see the moon and stars at
night, or the sun sparkling on the water,
when you hear birds singing in the trees,
when you hear the song of creation, then
the gift of caring will be born to you.

On the path of emptiness, you will remember
when you ate the fruit and felt different. When
things go wrong, when no one understands
you, when you lose the things you love, when
you feel sad, lonely or frightened, then the gift
of learning will be born to you.

On the path of making, you will remember the song that is inside you. When you have good ideas, when you make something beautiful,

when you tell stories and sing my song, then the gifts of learning and caring will start to grow.

On the path of coming home, you will remember that you are part of everything. When you look after the Earth, when you defend the helpless, when you speak for those that have no voice, when you enjoy and respect my creation, then you will be most like me. Your learning and caring will shine out everywhere. You will be separate no more.'

'Must we leave our home and all we love?' cried the Man and the Woman.
'All places are your home. Everything I have made is your family,' said God.
'Must we leave you?' cried the Man and the Woman.
'I will always be with you on your journey,' God promised.

'Will we really find the gift of learning and caring?' asked the Man and the Woman.

God said, 'Yes. You ate the fruit of the Tree of Life before it was ripe. But the seeds of learning and caring will grow inside you.'

And God blessed them both,
saying 'I will ripen your gift as you
walk the paths of light. Your gift will be a
blessing seed. It will leap from your hearts into
the hearts of others. Go now and spread my
blessing throughout the Earth.'

'Will we really find the gift of learning and caring?' asked the Man and the Woman.

God said, 'Yes. You ate the fruit of the Tree of Life before it was ripe. But the seeds of learning and caring will grow inside you.'

And God blessed them both,
saying 'I will ripen your gift as you
walk the paths of light. Your gift will be a
blessing seed. It will leap from your hearts into
the hearts of others. Go now and spread my
blessing throughout the Earth.'

The Man and the
Woman thanked God.
They walked out into the
wide world, taking the
blessing seed in their hearts.

Author's Note

Creation stories throughout the world speak of a paradisal time of bliss when things were perfect. Usually something happens to break the charmed circle and everyday life as we know it begins its long, downward spiral.

The biblical narrative myth of the creation has always both fascinated and worried me. It is significant that most people know this story as 'The Fall' rather than 'The Creation'. As the common heritage of the Jewish and Christian traditions, this story, literally interpreted, has been applied by clerics to control people and dictate how they run their lives. The resulting sense of blame, shame and guilt has frequently left a legacy of hopelessness and unhappiness in many hearts. It has also contributed to a high-handed disregard of the natural world and sometimes to a dismaying hatred of life itself.

Because the Bible starts with the Book of Genesis, its readers have assumed that this creation story was written down before the other books of the Bible. This is not actually the case. The creation narrative arrived a long time after the Pentateuch, and incorporates earlier Sumerian creation epics and other features of Jewish mystical philosophy. If we examine these sources, we find a different slant to the story, which I have hinted at in *The Blessing Seed*.

Jewish mystical tradition speaks of the Shekinah, the female companion of God, who 'moved on the face of the waters' during the creation of the world. It is she who accompanies Adam and Eve when they leave the Garden of Eden and for whom their descendants attempt to create a dwelling place in their hearts. From the evidence of early Christian Gnosticism and the post-exile texts of the Bible, we similarly see the figure of Sophia, or Wisdom, as the female companion who labours to bring humankind to knowledge of the Divine.

In both Jewish and Gnostic mysticism, there is the notion of the Tikkun or Apocatastasis – a time of mending, when the scattered or disconnected fragments of the original creation are brought into harmony again. This is a feature totally absent from the canonical biblical creation story, although it can be discovered in other parts of the Bible and in the parallel sources of the mystical Jewish and Christian traditions.

As we enter a new millennium, it seems timely that all of us, Christians or not, should reassess our ideas about our role as human beings in an increasingly fragile world, replacing the notion of original sin with one of 'original blessing'.

In writing *The Blessing Seed*, I have been particularly conscious of the way in which children consider stories in the context of their own lives: how we return to our source when things have gone wrong is an important thing to learn when we are young. The song of creation in this story reminds us to reconnect with the deep well of life. The blessing seed roots in each of us: if we walk the fourfold pathway of life, that seed will grow into a mighty tree in whose branches the Great Spirit can live and flourish.

Caitlín Matthews

BAREFOOT BOOKS publishes high-quality picture books for
children of all ages and specialises in the work of artists and writers from
many cultures. If you have enjoyed this book and would like to receive a copy of
our current catalogue, please contact our London office — tel: 0171 704 6492
fax: 0171 359 5798   email: sales@barefoot-books.com
website: http://www.barefoot-books.com